# FATHERHOOD AT 19...
# NO TUTORIAL BOOKS

A memoir by Curtis L. Witters

Published by Curtis L. Witters
Lil Villa Publishing
www.Fatherhoodat19.com

# Edited By Curtis L. Witters & Naomi B. Lynch

For all booking or inquiries for "Fatherhood at 19…No Tutorial Books" contact the author via email: Fatherhoodat19ntb@gmail.com

Cover Design: Black Encryption Designs-theblackdistrict.com

ISBN: 978-1-7350063-4-5

# DEDICATION

Since you brought me into this world you have nurtured my mind, body and soul. You have giving me strength and guided me through some of the most trying moments in my life. You always serve as my beacon of light, my inspiration, my influence and with GOD's will, I pray to be blessed with the strength, wisdom and determination I have witness you exhibit. There is nothing in this life I will not accomplish!

I dedicate this memoir to you Ma! I love
you with all my being Jazzy!

# Acknowledgments

First and foremost I can't go any further without acknowledging the power of GOD in my life. I am blessed to be fortunate enough to be in the graces of The Most High and receive his blessings. Everything in my life is only possible through the presence of The Most High. I continue to pray that you offer me everything you see fit to continue to be the best Father, Husband, Son, Brother, Uncle, Friend and Businessmen I could possibly be.

To my children Jaishaun, Keyshawn & Makazia... the blessing of having you all as my children has evolved me in ways I could never imagine. Every breath I'm giving I believe strongly it is for the purpose of offering you all a better way of life. You three are my world & the only way I could offer this memoir is because I was giving the honor & blessing of being y'all father. Love you all!

To my wife who is my Goddess, I would like to thank you for being the women you are. You always inspire me to be the best man I can possibly be! I'm honored to share the responsibility of raising our beautiful, gifted children together. Love you!

To my parents who have invested and contributed to my well being even till this day, I want to say thank you for sacrificing to make sure I've become the man you all see in me. My mother Jazzy & Poppa Doc, My father King R & Mama Eunice, Aunties, Uncles, Cousins, Nieces, Nephews and siblings, Ebony, WY, Sha Baby, James, & Michael. I am grateful for having you all in my life because it shows me the true wealth I am blessed with.

To my brother and business partner M-One Six, you always in my corner and in the battlefield with me getting work done! Love you for that bro. Brother Life thank you for pushing me to always do the best! My brother and business partner Mr. Professional the other half of Office Boys NY we see it in our mind, we will it and push that power! Thank you brother! My brother P. Bombay always in my corner for whatever is needed and always ready to contribute to the vision TW brother! (We In the Office). My brother-in-law CM Dubb, since we linked from Jansport days we always pushed each other to be better! I appreciate you for that bro.

To both my fathers, I thank you for contributing a part of yourself to make me who I am. Poppa Doc you taught me what it is to be an honorable stand up man and I'm forever appreciative for you accepting me as your son! Salute! To King R, we knew from the gate that we would not live according to society but according to GOD. That has allowed us to receive all the blessings that The Most High intended! Thank you for receiving me in your life when your son needed you most.

To some of my closet friends who have become my extended family who may also serve as spiritual advisers, motivational sources and the ultimate briefcase support. I just want to say that I appreciate and thank you for valuing my friendship. Auntie Di, Wopo Freshh, Phillip Pitts, Mark Davis, Redd Traumas, Madd Mann, Mr. HD, John Bibbs (Chi Town), M Vello, Cary Grant, Angie from Brooklyn. Tammie Bella, Author Untamed, Donnell Watkins of Distinguished Gentlemen, Baby Diamond Sis Author Vulyncia, LaDonna Marie, Kiana Donae, Ms. Lynn, Dana Haawa and Mr. & Mrs. Tucker.

To Black District of Black Encryptions! Brother this is one of the opportunities I get to let the world know how talented you are and also let the world know that you are a real brother! Thank you for taking the time to contribute your craft to my first book project. You always do superb work and I genuinely thank you for the impressive work on the book cover! You can never go wrong with Black Encryptions.

To one of my new found lil sisters Naomi B. Lynch, thank you for not hesitating since the first day we met and realizing the jewel I possessed when it came to this memoir. Thank you for your patience and your countless effort to bring the memoir to a place where I know the message can be received without any distractions taking away from it.

To a few Kings unknown to them, are the Fathers who have inspired me since a young man. It is through your diligence as Fathers that I began to see living examples of what a Father should be. My Great Grandfather Sharpie Rogers, (R.I.P.) My Grandfather James Rogers (R.I.P.), OG Sean Du (R.I.P.), you were one of the living examples I seen outside of my family in the Ville being a stand up Father. Kenneth Wilson, Poppa Perci, Mr. Bowe, OG Big Mike, My Cousin Redd, My Cousin Carl "Big C", Poppa Wilson (R.I.P. you always treated me like a Son), Poppa L's (R.I.P.) Mr. Thomas (Thank you for always taking the time to build!), Mr. Dugger (R.I.P.) and Mr. Tucker. To my uncle Curt, I got to see first hand the love a Father can show his son, thank you.

To my uncle Keith, before you had your own sons the bond you built with me already let me know you would be the great Father you are today. To Uncle Kenny & Uncle Junior, thank you for being examples of what it means to be your own man. You two never hesitated to build with me and that goes on till this day.

Last but never least, to my brother, business partner and right hand... Roland "King Tuck" Tucker Jr. It's not a day that goes by that I wish you was here to breathe these accomplishments with me! Since we linked in B More, you would have thought we grew up from Pre K together. You pushed me when other people wouldn't, you contributed whatever you had to move the company forward and I won't stop till we knock down all the goals we built about! (R.I.P. Tuck) we still Lil Villa Pubbing!

To anyone else who I may have forgotten to mention whether it is family or friends just know that I genuinely thank you all from my heart and soul. Enjoy!

# *Introduction*

A man can live in the ways of any religion but, if there is no direct connection to God or no transition to establish one, there is no obligation to principles, morals, or purpose to nurture, raise and guide their own lives, let alone another.

In the experiences, opinions, stories and different perspectives I share with you all in this memoir, please understand that it took me some time to accept God in my life; yet at a young age, it allowed me to become a better man in so many ways. It also keeps me humble enough to know that with every breath I'm granted I must strive to be better not just for myself...but also for the extensions the Lord has allowed me to create in my life.

I thank you, Lord; for the human you have created me to be and the human you've allowed me to become. PRAISES DUE!

# SHORT BIOGRAPHY

S haring my personal life has never been a big thing for me. Never am I ashamed of my family or who I am, I tend to just look at things from a protective mindset.

I'm the oldest of five siblings: two brothers and a sister from my mother's side of my creation, and two sisters from my father's side of my creation. Being a big brother definitely shaped the foundation for being a Father in more ways then I would know in my life.

Since I had a hand in raising my little brothers and sister, I relied on those experiences when it came time for me to raise my own children: my daughter and my two sons.

When I share some of the experiences from my childhood, most ask: "Do you feel robbed of your childhood?" And I would say no, although I was a young cat taking on some heavy responsibilities.

As the older brother, taking care of my siblings at a young age gave me an early sense of pride, purpose and manhood. As an adult, I appreciate now that my mom didn't raise me to take the place of my father, to be the man of the house. She raised me with the belief that someday I will be a man taking care of and providing order in my own household.

In holding down my moms with the house, of course there were times I wanted to play outside with no cares in the world. My care tended to change a little bit when I saw the determination, sac-rifice and dedication my mom put into raising us. I felt it was my duty as her eldest child to be the one she can depend on to help her through whatever may come.

During the younger years of my childhood, my father made the decision to go his way and leave me to walk my journey as a young man alone, without the guidance of the man I would depend on most. So, I would see him in spurts leading up to me becoming a teenager.

I remember being a little angry in my early years. There was one instance when my father was scheduled to come pick me up, then abruptly called saying he couldn't come... I just went off! I went to my room, threw shit around, kicked things over, and turned my music up! My cool cat of an Uncle, Uncle C, used some of his joking ways to calm me down but it still stung like a bee that my father didn't come get me. It started to feel like he didn't want to chill with me.

It was at that moment that my moms took the opportunity to put me in check and also instilled in me the lessons of not taking things out on others, and addressing the root of that problem: The feeling that my father didn't want me.

I can truly say, that as I was growing up my mother never threw any dirt on my father's name. She always allowed me to see my father through not just his own words but also his actions. The more I began to understand that, the more I understood that any issues that needed to be expressed with him or anyone should be addressed with said person.

As I began to share and reflect on my childhood experiences, I couldn't lie and say I had a crazy, malnourished childhood -- that was far from the truth. My mom has, and continues to be, a queen, who has raised us in the honorable ways of life. Whatever may have transpired in her relationship with my father, as well as my sibling's father was none of my business, and she didn't allow me to make that my business, unless they were causing her harm. My mother will never be anyone's doormat.

The experiences I had in regards to fatherhood in my adolescence were rich but distant at times. My uncle C, who I mentioned earlier, raised his son by himself. My cousin didn't have his mother around when he was younger. So I got to see some examples of fatherhood on a day to day, when my uncle and cousin lived with us for a while. Principles were set and accountability was present. Despite whatever it was people attached to my uncle's name, being a good Father are one of them.

In most of my adolescent experiences, manhood was attached to fatherhood because in each instance the Father would share a piece of who he was as a man, or how he became a man through his words, actions, or experiences. Besides my uncle that I just mentioned, I have a few men who would contribute to my ideal of manhood.

I am fortunate to say that some of my most important jewels I was given as a young man have come from my great grandfather Sharpie. His talks were key in me understanding my manhood and how it goes hand in hand with fatherhood.

My great-grandfather Sharpie Rogers was a great man, not just because of who he was and how he took care of his family, but how he was a Father to not just his own children but children in his community. I remember going to visit my father and him being preoccupied with his drinking, so I waited for him at my great-grandfather Sharpie's house. We would have these sit downs that would help mold my young mind.

Sharpie would share stories with me about how he grew up and the importance of working hard. He, as well as my uncle, would also cultivate my mind to appreciate young ladies. I laugh at some of the teasing I used to get...

*"How many girlfriends you got boy"...*
*"You got that Rogers blood in ya, I know they*
*on ya".*

To some this may be interpreted as raising a young man to treat ladies as objects but this did the complete opposite for me. See, I'm blessed to have special bonds with some of my family members. My aunts offered me advice from a woman's perspective and the men in my life helped me to understand and apply the lessons. So I have the utmost respect for the estrogen species on many levels. This connection and learning from both sexes in my family, allowed my mind to start shaping what type of young lady I would want for my spouse and based on what I learned from these examples in my life, I started to think on who will I be as a man. What would my contributions be once I am blessed with the gift of fatherhood?

Before I take you deeper into my beliefs and concepts of fatherhood as well as my relationships with my father I would like to offer you this.

It is an expression that is often thrown around and it goes "a woman can't raise a boy to be a man". Now in a lot of ways this is logical, but when you are blessed with a Mother like mine you can poke holes in that notion. No, my mom didn't teach me how to bounce a basketball or how to hold myself when using the bathroom -- Although I learned quickly not to leave the toilet seat up --but what my beautiful Mom did do was encourage and cultivate the man that was growing in me. It takes a special woman to understand that as a woman, no she can not teach me what my father was supposed to teach me, but she did know that it was her duty to guide me and allow me to shape my own ideals of the man I wanted to be. For this she has gifted her son in many ways, I love her tremendously for this.

My mother never allowed me to think that anything outside of being a young man was cool like playing with baby dolls or wearing feminine clothing. She couldn't tell me from a man's perspective how and what it takes to be a good man but what she did do was teach me what a man should be from a powerful women's perspective.

# FATHER FIGURE

As I offer my thoughts, experiences and opinions, I'm sure it is safe to say that we all agree that "Father figure" is not a term to be used loosely to describe any man who has a child.

Father figures are men who have accepted their responsibilities, fulfill their obligations raising their children and lead a progressive life for the sake of themselves as well as their children.

Again the fatherhood factor was faint in my life in my early adolescence. I never kept it a secret that I didn't grow up with my father through my youth. We didn't establish a powerful bond until I was sixteen. Throughout my youth I would see him occasionally. At times I remember being cool with that...then it was times I felt it was necessary for him to be there. In all honesty until we established our bond I had a few examples of male figures that helped me strive to be a young man of honor as well as keep me in line.

A rich adolescence is what I was blessed with and no I'm not talking about any material riches. What I'm speaking of is family from my Grandma Ann and Grandpa Willie (*God Bless them, R.I.P*) to my great Grandfather Sharpie and great Grandmother Nana (God Rest their souls R.I.P.). A tribe of aunts, along with family had a lot to do with weaving the fabric of who I would become. Although my dad was distant during these times, his family had a great impact on my life and still does. They didn't establish a bond with me through my father, because they took it upon themselves to build with me directly and I will always love them for that.

In the mid-80s my mom left my sibling's Dad. He had his demons that led to my mom having to make that tough decision to leave. Later I would realize it wasn't just for my mother's safety and well being, but the safety and well being of her kids as well.

Jim Bo used to be a good dude in my eyes. I learned a little hustling through watching some of his moves as a youngster. He used to hustle women's clothes, work a job and Lord knows what else to take care of us, but he held it down. When his demons began to make themselves present on a day to day I guess my mom felt it was enough.

The switch to young manhood happened when I realized that Jim Bo and Mom were getting to a place where things were not going to be the same. With Jim Bo being gone out of the house my mom would not fall victim to waiting on anyone providing for her or her children so she got a night job at the post office. Being the oldest, plus having the bond that my mom and I have, she started to put her trust in me a little more. She began to teach me the things I needed to know to hold the household down while she was working to take care of us.

At this same time I began to develop what I believe was a protection complex: if none of these two men that my mom shared her life with would hold us down, then it was my job as the oldest child to make sure she would not raise our family by herself. When that notion hit, I went full blast. Although we lived upstairs from my auntie Bake cakes I was responsible for making sure my siblings ate, kept the house in order and giving them any assistance and support that my mom would provide.

It took some time but things were progressing and getting better for us without Jim Bo being there, but he would show up sometimes just to check in on us. He was really using that as an excuse to see what my mom was doing. Jim Bo saw that Mom was moving on without him and finally leading the life she wanted for her children-- and Jim Bo took that hard.

One night while my mom was getting ready to go to work my uncle Kenny had stopped by to pay us a visit. As my uncle was getting ready to wrap up his visit, my mom was getting ready to leave. As my uncle and mom are leaving, my uncle Kenny realizes that Jim Bo was at the gate with a knife behind his back, talking about he needed to speak with my mom.

My uncle Kenny was not a little guy and he is a smart brother. As this is going down I just remember this feeling of fear like...this mutha f*$*! Here to hurt my mom!" I did not know the first thing to do, but as I watched my uncle Kenny spring into action, I knew my job was to make sure my family is safe.

As my uncle Kenny walks towards Jim Bo he is talking to him and whatever my uncle says to him, it gets him to calm down and leave at this point. Then my uncle walks my mom to the train station to make sure she gets to work safely. After that experience I never felt the same about Jim Bo, it turned me cold to any dude that was not my family.

# FATHER FIGURE 2

My mom met "Poppa Doc" after working at the post office a year or so. Before my mom brought him around she spoke to us about him several times and let us know that he was a friend and if things did progress any further we were to remember that we always came first. I knew my mom meant that with every fiber of her being, what I didn't like was this new guy coming around...I didn't trust anybody.

The first time we met "Poppa Doc" that coldness I developed was beginning to surface and it was hard to hide it, I believe I was about 10 years old around this time. I felt my brothers and sister liked this man and that made me more upset for some reason. At this point in my young mind, I deemed this dude as not being worthy of my mother, and I began to express this every chance I got.

It was a couple instances that I took things to a level that I shouldn't have. One instance "Poppa Doc" was visiting and he brought all of us gifts. My siblings were excited, but in my mind I instantly thought: "This dude thinks he is going to buy me...hell na...watch this." Concrete floor, meet Walkman. Walkman, meet floor.

My mother was very upset at me, because she felt that me being the oldest I needed to set a better example for my siblings and if I acted like this, they would follow. After some time my siblings began to warm up to him. For me, as cool as "Poppa Doc" was, my young mind did not want to compromise the position I thought I was holding in the family because I felt no one was worthy of my mom's love because of the hurt I witnessed her go through.

As my mom began to grow closer to him, I thought to myself: "Why couldn't my father get this right and be here?" That only made me act out more. Sometime went by, when one weekend "Poppa Doc" had us over his apartment for the weekend and made us some breakfast. My siblings and I were in his bedroom eating breakfast and watching TV and I was still on my bullsh*t. I bashed my brothers and sister: "Y'all falling for this dude?" They contested of course and asked me why I didn't just let things be. I couldn't let things be.

My whole goal was to scare "Poppa Doc" off so that we could go about our family business without him. I felt that we didn't need him. As time would tell it I was wrong. From the way things were going "Poppa Doc" was going nowhere. He really loves us.

At the time what my siblings said upset me so I took my breakfast and dumped my eggs in his sock draw. As an adult now I know I was totally out of line for that but when you're a young man going through some life transitions like this, respectable actions escaped my thoughts sometimes.

One thing I could say is that even as my mom got closer to "Poppa Doc" she never closed us out. As things began getting really serious between them, one day she sat my siblings and I down to explain to us that he loved all of us and how he was going to be in our lives. Being that he was going to be in our lives she needed me to get to a better space about him now being the man of the house. My mom expressed to me whatever issues I had with "Poppa Doc" I needed to get over it because he only has my best interests at heart.

By this time a couple of years had passed and as I was getting older. My mom's happiness meant a lot to me and I did not want to get in the way of that. So I began to ease up on the bullsh*t because "Poppa Doc" showed me through his actions he was a man of honor and respect. He would take care of those he considered his family and his actions definitely supported that.

# FATHER FIGURE 3

Although things began to get a lot better between "Poppa Doc" and I, I was beginning to go through a lot of different things as I was turning into a teenager. Puberty, girls, getting to know who I was and everything else that accompanies being a young "black" male growing up in Brooklyn.

During this time I had sporadic contact with my father. He would come through a few times with a bike or some clothes, which I loved, but it would never replace the feeling of wanting my father around on a daily basis. So I still found myself acting out at times because I didn't know how to deal with the emotions I was going through.

I'm now 15 and "Poppa Doc" had been living with us now for some time and although it was apparent that he was helping my mom take care of the household, I still kept a wall up, thinking if I kept my distance in some ways I would never be hurt by him or anyone because I was always guarded.

Unfortunately I took a complete turn in the opposite direction of how my mom raised us. I began to find myself in trouble here and there. Due to my own poor decisions I found myself locked up facing charges for assault and robbery.

I spent a couple of days in jail and thought I was going to be in there longer when they gave me bail where my parents had to come up with $3,000 to get me out. It was this moment that I felt "Poppa Doc" really cared about me because he got up the bail money for me.

That moment showed me he was willing to do whatever was needed of him because he really started to embrace us as not just his lady's children but also that of his own.

After going back to court, then heading back to Spofford, my name was called right before I would head back to my cell. When I got home my mother had a few choice words for me, but I just felt good that I was home. Next morning my mom leaves for work and "Poppa Doc" comes in from work. I thought it would be the regular routine of him sending a message through my mom, but this was about to change.

A few hours after being home "Poppa Doc" came into my room and began to give me the business. He asked, "You want to be a man? You think you tough out here, you want to run away, you out here getting locked up...let me show you what it is to be a tough guy." He snatched me up by my collar. He told me "I thought you were a leader, I thought you were about making your mother proud but all you are doing is hurting her heart and I will not tolerate this!"

After that clash with "Poppa Doc" I started to think hard about the things I was doing and the way I was affecting the household.

After I assessed a few things, I knew I was wrong but I did not know how to deal with the things I was going through. My mom and I relationship had always been super glue tight. In my mind, some of that closeness had changed because my mom now had someone else in her life that she could depend on and is there for her. I had to deal with that.

"Poppa Doc" is a very disciplined and honorable man. He was in the Navy, and he comes from a family that's about hard work, so he is a great example of what a man should be. In my younger years I didn't think "Poppa Doc" would be in our lives this long, but he turned out to be a blessing to the family. From a man's point of view, he was grooming us with the ideals our Fathers should have been teaching us to become exceptional humans.

Now that I reflect on the relationship I have with "Poppa Doc", he was one of the best things that happened in my life because, as I got older he showed me that a man has to be accountable for his actions. A man has to take responsibility for the decisions he makes and not pass the buck on anyone else for actions he has taken himself.

"Poppa Doc" taught me the importance of being a leader, taking care of the household first, and how to prioritize. He also taught me the importance of working hard toward your goals and something he would always say to me is "excuses are like assholes: everyone has one".

Some of these things I've learned from him would not reveal itself to me until later on in my adulthood, but the lessons I learned from him would be things I would use to measure myself as a man.

On the strength of that, I began to make gestures to show him that I got the lesson he was taking the time to teach. I began to show a lot more respect and appreciation to the contributions he has made to my life.

I remember this moment when we were all in the house having some family time. In the conversations we were having I realized we still referred to "Poppa Doc" by his first name. As we continued to converse, I thought to myself, "This man has been in our lives for a long while he married my mother and never labeled us as his "step children"-- why am I, as the oldest, not giving this man his just due?" He along with my mom had sacrificed a lot for us and still continued to do so.

It was at that moment that as the oldest I felt I needed to change things immediately... "YO POP".


Now keep in mind "Poppa Doc" is not big on emotion, especially with the boys, but the day I referred to him as "Pop" along with my siblings, I think he understood that we fully accepted him as our father and needed him to know that we love and appreciate him.

Later down the line my mom shared with me that "Poppa Doc" held that moment close to his heart and that moment played a part in solidifying his place in our family.

"Poppa Doc" has always and will always be a prime example of what a Father is and how a man should carry himself to not only care for, but also how to protect his family.

In me sharing my ideals of fatherhood with you all, I felt it was very necessary to share how important "Poppa Doc" is and how he would become more than a Father figure to me. How through his actions he took on the responsibility of being a Father to my siblings and I. For that he will always be that dude to us.

Now although "Poppa Doc" is known as the man who took care of us and held the position of being the Father figure in our lives, my mother continued to never throw any dirt on any of our father's names. Again, she allowed their own actions to speak for themselves.

# FATHER FIGURE 4

 I'm now getting further in my teenage years and it's been some time since I have seen my father. Things were fine at my mother's house but I was battling through some things in my own mind as I was breathing in my teenage years. An opportunity for me to do something further with my music career came about that I felt I needed to do. When Mom and Poppa Doc wouldn't sign off on it, I felt it was time for me to take things into my own hands. I went to my girl's house after running away from home to tell her what I was doing, and then I proceeded to make my way to my father's house where he lived in Bushwick on Pilling Street at the time.

 Ring! Ring...moments later my father and stepmom come to the door. "HEYYYYYYYY!" They greeted me with mad love. My little sister came downstairs, while my baby sis was in my stepmom's arms.

 They invite me in. We kicked it for a while and then my father asks, "What's up son; I see you have bags. How long are you stay-ing?" I look at him for a little while and say, "It may be a while, Pops." My father and Mama Eunice gave each other a look as if to say, "What did he say?" As Mama Eunice leaves the room so my father and I can talk, he turns to me and asks, "What's really going on here?" Before I even get a word in, he says, "Does your mother know you are here?"

From there, the can of worms was opened.

My father and I talked for a little while. He tells me "First thing you need to do is call your mother to let her know where you are. I'm going to go talk to my wife, but you call your mama!"

As I made my way to the phone I got super hot...big beads of sweat started forming, I was not ready to let my mother know what was going on...but I had to. When I started dialing the buttons it felt like slow motion and when my mother picked up I could already hear the tears forming.

*"Where are you, Curtis?" she asks.*
*"Ma, I'm at my dads house," I answer*
*"So what's going on you leave here, you don't tell me what's going on, your things are gone... are you going to live with your father?"*
*"Yes Ma I'm going to be here for a while." I say.*
*"Well Curtis, you go ahead and live with your father if you think that he can do better for you, and you want to live like you're grown, go ahead Curtis!"*

My mom got so mad that she pushed the phone to "Poppa Doc" and didn't want to speak to me anymore. I was crushed but I knew my mother was hurt deeply.

A couple of days went by and it was decided that I was going to stay there at my father's house for a while. Now I'm thinking, time to put my plan in motion it's time to push the button and see if my father is going to give me the green light to go to Canada. Talk about being determined to move on a plan, this is the reason why I bounced from my mother's house because they didn't sign off on me moving on what I believe to be a big opportunity for me.

I bring up the plan to my father and he says "What! ...You are going out there to do what, with whom? Check this out first we got to talk about this and if I do let you go I need to meet these cats face to face".

I worked every pitch I could to get them to let me make this move and guess what, they decided I could go. Of course with a few stipulations but I was on the way to riding to another country to follow my visions.

It was very important for me to share this story about this trip to Canada to record this demo under this management agreement for several reasons. The main reason being it was one of the first major decisions my father has made in my life within a matter of a few days of me living with him. Secondly, It was one of the first major steps for my father and I to build a relationship that involved him in my life on a day-to-day basis, as well as him supporting my aspirations like my mother does.

As I lived at my father's house, I began to realize that running away from my mom's house was a small percentage of me not liking their rules there, because they gave me room as a young man. It was more about the things that were going on in my life at the time. I needed my father to contribute to my life more than some school clothes or a bike or a once in a blue moon visit.

# MY BIOLOGICAL POPS

My dad was not totally absent from my young life. From time to time he would come scoop me up, take me to his house for the weekend and take me around to see the other side of my family. This is another extension of the richness that I have in my life.

When my aunties and uncles would reach out to me -- especially my Auntie Desiree and my Auntie Di, they always wanted me to know that regardless of my relationship I had with my father, I was very much loved by them as well.

When I was younger and learned my father had problems with alcohol, I realized this also played a role with how our relationship was, and how he dealt with me. I began to understand it was a disease that my father would have to tackle on his own with us offering any support he needed. That journey that I witnessed my father go through is one of the examples that helped me to understand that if a man really wanted to change for the better, he could but…that change would first have to be strengthened by GOD and then embraced by man.

My mom and "Poppa Doc" did a powerful job raising me to understand my responsibilities as a man. It was just a time in my life where GOD knew I needed to see and know the man I emerge from to understand the man I needed to be.

As a young man, it was only a few things I knew about my father and him being a nice basketball player was one of them. Being "The Man" was another thing I knew of him. In my younger years he kept a gold can of beer in his hand ("Old E" to be exact), but in the same breath it's many more layers to my father that I needed to see and experience for myself.

For any young man I feel it's imperative to know who his Father is as a man, not just Dad. I feel getting to know this side of the man who helped bring me into this world gives me an idea of who I am and who I can be. Their faults, strengths, plights, losses, successes, failures, tribulations and triumphs help give us insight as to who we are. Although the way I may have gone about it was hurtful to my mother, it allowed me the time to get to know not only my father better, It also helped me learn more about myself.

This allowed my father and I the time to build a stronger bond and gain clarity as to where we both were in our lives and how we needed each other in these particular times in our lives. Only God presented the opportunity for that and I believe it was none other than God's plan for us to build our relationship in this manner.

The bond I would build with my father at this point in my life wasn't about us doing what was right under society's perspective. This was about my father and I not allowing the past to hold us hostage or dictate the bond we needed to have to move in the future for the sake of both of us.

The time I spent with my father allowed me to learn lessons hands on in regards to being a man. I learned things from having a dedicated work ethic, to receiving respect from the streets, to people who ran offices. I also learned my father's position amongst his siblings growing up as a child and him always referred to as a protector, or the person who would go out of his way to do what was needed for his family.

That helped me begin to identify with the traits I exhibited in regards to my overprotective mind state. When I was with him - whether it was going to his job or walking to the store he was always greeted and shown respect from people of all different walks of life. Not every man is the same, so to see your father walk the path as a man is to see himself as he is giving the opportunity to learn, apply, and be greater than the man which contributed to his existence.

Having the opportunity to see my father interact with his own father, and his father's father gave me a glance at what I should be extending to my sons when I became a Father. Not just the ideals of being a man but the actions I saw them practice.

When I was afforded the moments to hang with my great-Grandfather, Grandfather and my father ... these were the moments when I was gaining my rights of passage as a young man.

From time to time my father shared bits and pieces of his relationship with his father. In most of the accounts he shared with me, my Grandfather wasn't so easy going in raising and disciplining him during his childhood. Again as I began to learn more of my father's experiences with his own father, new perspectives began to enter my mind as to the reason why our relationship as Father and Son was what it was. This is what kept feelings of bitterness at bay. In my mind it was logic, how can someone give something that they are not sure whether they have it in them to give.

This was a prime example of a man: In this case, my father being conscious of how he grew up with his father and possibly being in a space where he didn't want to pass on some of the things he experienced in his relationship with his father to the relationship with his son. I began to understand my father could only offer me what he experienced from his father and what was in his heart to give.

My father was raised to be tough like his Dad; he wasn't raised to be no sucker. Naturally, he passes that on to me, but through his own personal experiences I believe the compassion he may not have gotten from his Dad was something he desired to share with me based on the lack of it from his Dad when he was young. During this time of me living with my father I also learned resilience. I witnessed some of his moments in AA meetings where he shared his pain, tribulations and the mistakes he made in his life based off of the decisions he has made under the influence of alcohol, and how he was going to do what was necessary to make the change to make things better in his life. He also acknowledged how this is something he had to take a day at a time.

Well I was watching him take things in life a day at a time and I watched how he built himself to be stronger than he was in previous years. Now the man that was always in him has emerged based on him taking the time to recognize the weakness that was building destruction in him and him shedding the habits that indulge his lesser self.

Being there at that time in his life allowed me to witness these things firsthand. In witnessing some of that healing and growing I also learned that my forgiveness contributed to his transition of being a greater him. At this stage in my life learning everything I was from GOD, my biological father and my stepfather, I began to really start to make solid decisions as to who I would be as a man and a Father.

# DECISION TO BE A FATHER

The act of making love is one of the most beautiful sensations in this GOD giving life of ours in my opinion. As I got more into my adulthood, it was clear to me that the "love instruments" and emotions we are giving is way more important and powerful than we know.

Even though I considered myself as a young man who some of the ladies were fond of, when I was in my teens, I was blessed with the discipline to not stick my love muscle in every young tender who winked her eyes at me.

That may sound strange coming from a young man, but then again since my early teenage years I believed I knew what I wanted in a woman. Don't get me wrong -- I had my share of rendezvous and misguidance, but I quickly began to understand the responsibility that came with being sexually active and depositing baby juice into a women's nature space.

The examples of great women in my life happened since birth. For me to be brought into the world through the most beautiful human I know, my mother set the bar high for me. No, I did not want a woman that was just like my mom, I just prayed for a woman who embodied some of the qualities my mother has.

Now between my Grandmother, Mom and Aunties I was given examples of how a woman should carry herself, the love she should have for herself and the qualities she should possess. Not only that, I had the benefit of learning how to communicate with a woman and the first lessons I learned were listening with my ears, not my mouth.

All these lessons from a young man all up into my adulthood helped to give me a sense of the women I would want to occupy my time and build with.

As I was growing up my interest was not to have a "baby mother" and add to the cycle of raising children in broken homes so I really took the time to try to understand any woman I would see myself hugging and loving because mistakes happen, as well as love. Having a child with a woman whom I considered capable of raising a family was very important to me...yes, even at a young age.

I had these thoughts about the type of woman I wanted to conceive a child with, but I did not plan what age I wanted to be a Father. I know I wanted to first accomplish the goals I set for myself and put myself in a position where I can take care of a family.

The way I was planning on living, thoughts of having a child seemed like it would come later on in my life, but the universe showed me otherwise. I met a young lady who would become the Mother of my children when I was 15 years old in Brownsville, Brooklyn, where I believed my adolescence accelerated.

My mindset even at that time in my life was a few years ahead of the average teenager. I knew I was going to have a successful career in business and music, so I wanted a woman who knew and loved me before I got exposed to the people who would just rock with me because of who I became. It took me a little time to realize it but the women I needed in my life to accomplish my family goals, was gifted to me.

I wouldn't advise any young man to move in with his girlfriend at 17 years old like I did because playing house and taking care of the house are two different things. My rib was very centered on taking care of business because some early life changes accelerated her maturity as well. I like to refer to my wife as my rib because I felt in what I ask for from GOD in a woman, she was gifted to me.

At first I was very reluctant to move in with my rib because I felt I needed to experience my own space for a while before sharing a space with her. A lot of life changing things was going on in her life at the time. In her sharing what was going on, I felt as if I did go my own route and not hold this young lady up; she would have really been in the world by herself and getting to know her more made it clear to me that we were brought together for a reason, a reason bigger than we both knew.

Of course moving in with my girl at 17 years old was exciting I was able to go and come as I pleased, I now had what is known as "In-house" (*for those who don't know it's loving whenever you wanted because you lived with your companion*) and the freedom to begin to build my life how I wanted it to be. Once you get through the stage of "living it up", as you want for the first couple of months you are quickly hit with the reality of not only having your own space but also maintaining it. With living with my rib at this age it allowed us the time to really get to know each other and I was very impressed with how she orchestrated things in our first apartment.

My maturity level only complemented hers because she would respect my suggestions and the order I contributed to the household as well. Learning this aside from knowing how compassionate, nurturing and loving my rib is I began to feel a sense of this is the woman I may have been blessed with to build my family.

Now part of my thought process was to get to know the woman I would procreate with on as many levels as possible. In beginning to learn my rib physically, spiritually, and mentally, knowing how she was raised was important for several reasons. One of the reasons my rib's upbringing was important to me is because

I wanted to make sure that not only I could contribute to their childhood progressively, she would be able to contribute in a healthy way as well.

Unfortunately, My rib's childhood was not anything she would have liked it to be because of some of the issues that face many of our homes like alcohol abuse, drug abuse, and domestic violence. In many cases this has led to families being broken up and children being raised in foster care. Learning about how my rib was raised, the things she endured and to see the love she still had inside of her allowed me to see how much love she wanted to give to her own children. It allowed me to see what she was willing to invest into raising our children.

She deserved to experience that and it gave me an overwhelming feeling as to her being the woman who I would share the investment of love, nurturing and happiness to building a family we both would be proud of.

Reflecting on this now, our first son was born a year and a few months from us moving in together and in all honestly I could confess to you that the bond that my rib and I built led us to deciding it was time to share a child together.

Ideally we would all like to have our children born at the perfect time with financial security and stability in our lives, but there is nothing like being blessed to know that everything you need to be a successful parent is within you and comes from GOD first. The rest will appear based on you as an individual. You have to feel the need to build a cohesive parenting bond to raise the child to be the best human possible.

Taking the time to learn about the woman I would share the responsibility of raising children with, was half of what I based the decision to become a father on. The other half of the decision was taking the time to learn more about myself.

There were a few men in my life like my uncle Kenny, and one of my older cousin Red who would introduce me to not only books, but offer conversations that sparked my interest to become more knowledgeable as to what a man is, the importance of knowing God and having knowledge in self. This was key in becoming a Father because a man has to know what he is capable of, how to earn to take care of a child, and how to build a solid foundation for a family to stand on. To do that, it starts with a man having knowledge and building up himself.

Once I began to understand this and get an idea of the things I would need to continuously grow to become a Father, a calm went over my physical being. I began to reflect on moments helping raise my sister and brothers, having a small sense of the responsibility that is needed to raise a child. Although I was 18 about to be 19 years old, age didn't matter to me anymore in regards to having a child.

The fact that I felt I could contribute to the well being of a life I brought in the world was good enough for me at that moment. I felt that when fatherhood happens, I would be ready to embrace all that fatherhood has in store for me.

# BECOMING A FATHER

Maybe it's just me, but I strongly feel there is a difference between having sex with your partner and conceiving a child. I haven't shared this with anyone and I feel it's only right at this moment to share with you all that during the point of making love to my then girlfriend who is now my wife, the consummation that lead to my 1$^{st}$ born birth was like an outer body experience for me. I thought I could write the experience off as a different level of climax, but the days following the experience these feelings only grew.

When my rib thought she was pregnant the first time, she was disappointed, and I was too -- the test came back negative. After a few weeks had passed, she went to the doctors and got confirmation that she was pregnant. I was overwhelmed with different feelings. Nervousness, happiness, fear, joy, anticipation, love, uncertainty, doubts it was a lot going on. What I can say is that in that moment of going through all these emotions, calmness began to settle in me.

In the months leading to my sons' birth, as my rib's physical and emotional spaces were transforming, so was mine. I was gaining a little bit of "baby weight", but most of my transformation was happening in the mind. I began to reflect on my childhood and the things I didn't receive in my upbringing from my father. This is when I began to make vows to myself in regards to our unborn child because I remember repeating to myself I never wanted my son to feel what I felt growing up in the absence of my father.

Since 15 years old I had my first job and outside of never being scared to work, I also tended to have my hands in the concrete hustling anything from socks and incense to pounds and paint jobs.

The year leading up to my son's birth my balance between keeping a job and the streets, started leaning more towards the streets. The responsibility of maintaining our apartment and being an adult started driving me in a direction where whatever I need to do to take care of my rib, and I it was going to happen.

About three or four months into the pregnancy, I started to develop this coldness again that had my thoughts concerned with the only thing that mattered -- finding and maintaining ways to keep bread coming to the table. At this point in time I had two jobs, one in Long Island working a third shift then I would go to my morning job that was in a school in Brooklyn that my father connected me to. My rib was also working at this spot called Au Bon Pain where she was doing her thing well but she left around her 7th month because the pregnancy started to be a bit much for her.

When this happened it only sent me to overdrive and this is when I began to feel the real pressures of becoming a Father.

Now as I'm going through this period in my life, my father and I were building our relationship to be what it was going to be and not what it should be based on lost time. When I came to my father to live with him before this, he respected and met me in my space as a young man. I respected my father for him being there for me in the present and didn't attach myself to the "what ifs" of the past.

I offer you all this because it was in this time period I thought of him being right in my shoes. I began to see that it came down to the decision of being a Father is not only in the conception and action of making the child. The decision is also made in the process of the child coming into the world and providing the things that someone who chooses to be a Father invests himself in the wellbeing of his child. Sad to say, this is the harsh reality for a lot of children. Before my son was born, I realized the pressures of caring for someone regardless of your circumstances is the core of parenting.

This was in essence the space where most men folded to the pressures of maintaining a job and building a solid, respectable relationship with the women they're bringing a child into the world with. Now I have no choice but to present this reality as well. For some men and women, having a child may not have been a well thought out process or part of their plan at all. There was no decision to be made in regards to raising a family. In some cases the child was just a result of a chance sexual encounter or the evil of a woman's innocence being taken.

In the case where you are with someone you love and want to build a family, this is the time when you are going to have to make a solid decision, regardless of what the future holds... I am here to stand as my child's Father! Although I may face things that I'm ready for and not ready for, this child will always have me by their side to guide and take care of them to the very best of my abilities.

# HERE COMES JAI

Whew, I'm starting to get this tingling feeling just sharing this part of my son Jaishaun coming into the world cause as I write this, I'm on the other side of some of the things I thought we would never make it through. Pre birth, plus the last three months of the pregnancy were tribulations. My rib would have to endure the rest of the pregnancy at home to make sure his birth was good. I was more than willing to rise to the occasion and handle the home front. But the easy road I intended on gliding on had a few boulders on it.

I think it was the 6$^{th}$ or 7$^{th}$ month of my rib's pregnancy I got into a car accident. Because of the injuries I had to let one of the jobs go. The day job I was holding on to let me go to bring in some people who were more suitable for the job, people who they shared blood with. I didn't share blood with them so it was my time to go. At this point the only thing I felt I had left was my hand in the concrete. Due to the nature of my relationship with my rib she was never proud of me waving my hand in that direction but we were in the space of survival so she dealt with it.

I never put my rib in the mix of that. She always reminded me to stay on track and how I didn't need to get caught up in the streets because she didn't want to raise our son alone without me.

The time has come, or so we thought. One night, my rib starts to get these pains in her abdomen and says to me "Babes, it's time to go." I was knocked out cold from a long night of hustling. I hear my rib again "Babe I'm feeling contraction pains, it feels like he's coming out"

I say, "Babe you're ok; just think of a good place like the beaches and the ocean, you'll be fine." *My wife always reminds me of the story.* That might have worked for me but not for her; she started shaking me saying "This has nothing to do with beaches, it's time to go". I hopped up called my mom and told her to meet us at the hospital. Then I call my father to let him know it's time to come get us. It's 11pm on a Saturday night, my father pulls up like Leroy with warrants to the house. Then on the way to the hospital my father was gliding through lights and pulls up to the hospital like "Everybody better move: my Grandson on the way!"

After a quick visit with the doctor, we found out it was a false alarm. The doctor suggested I walk my rib around the hospital to help bring the baby further down. As my rib and I walk to the family to tell them what the word is, I began to see more examples outside of my rib and my Son as to why I have to be the best father I can possibly be. My mom, poppa doc, my father, mama Eu, my aunts and my cousin Red were right there. I'm getting this overwhelming feeling like my lady and I are not alone.

A few laps around the hospital and nothing, it was time to go back home. We nestled back in to get all cozy and sure enough, 4am Sunday morning... Sh*t gets real! The contractions this time will not be mistaken for a bluff move. So we press the button again and back to the hospital we go.

The doctor does his due diligence, measures my rib and says "Yep, she is at 10 centimeters, we're bringing your baby in the world today." I look my rib in her eyes and we are both nervous as a muthasucker the only comfort we find in that moment was holding hands. Now in your lifetime, GOD willing, you will have a lot of 1st time moments in your life. But I promise you the first time you see your child coming into the world, you will never experience a moment like that again.

After six hours of labor between home and the hospital, it was go time. I had previously got escorted out of the laboring room at Kings County because of the limited space and the screaming half-naked, laboring women sharing the room with my rib. I ended up pacing the hallway with my cousin Red until it was time for me to be called into the delivery room. I was considered a strong guy but beads of sweat started to slide down my back. My palms started sweating and in short... it was getting real, no turning back now.

Whether you're queasy or can handle the sight of blood well, I advise every man who has a child scheduled to come into the world to be there for the arrival of the child. As I was about to learn you don't want to have a child in this world and not experience the first moments of their lives.

As they began to push my rib into the delivery room, the doctor approached my cousin and I, telling my cousin Red "he'll be back, he has a baby to deliver today". I entered the prep room, scrubbed up and began to put on the delivery uniform.

On the way to the delivery room, the doctor asked, "Are you Dad? Are you going to cut the umbilical cord?" I reply "Yes I am, and hell yeah I want to cut the umbilical cord". We both smiled and proceeded to the delivery room where they already had my rib ready to go. As the delivery began I started to feel a warm tingly fill my body. Not the awe this is a warm moment, which it was, but dear lord what did I get myself into I'm about to see a whole human come out of this woman I have to get myself together type of warm.

"Breathe and push, Mom" says one of the nurses in the delivery room, as my rib obliges with a few heavy pushes. We do this several times and the more she pushes the more intense it gets, along with her manicure going deeper into my skin.

By now my clothes are moist from the sweat, my legs are wiggling a little bit and it feels like I'm going to go down because now I see a few hair follicles peeking from between my ribs thighs. Now the doctor requests a few steady consistent pushes and my rib obliges, pushing as hard as she can, I began to Jaishaun's face. As I feel myself getting sentimental I hear the doctor ask, "Dad are you ok." "Of course," I answer, "Yes, I'm all the way good Doc."

As the tears start draping down my eyes, I look up at my rib as she keeps pushing and she asks, " Do you see him?" I say, "Yes, I definitely do." She tells me she loves me and through the tears in my eyes, I see the doctor pulling Jai from the womb. Before I get a chance to wipe the tears the doctor hands me the scissors to cut the umbilical cord and says, "It's your turn, Dad."

With no hesitation, I cut Jai's umbilical cord and as I finished, blood squirts in my eye. Everyone asks if I'm ok and proceeded to clean off our son, while I'm standing in the delivery room frozen in a moment. To me this blood that just splash in my eye from my first-born is my seed anointing me as his father. Till this day that was one of the most AMAZING moments of my life. Although it burned a little the tears seem to dilute the blood that splashed in my eye.

"I'm officially a Father" I kept saying to myself as they were checking Jai's vitals and cleaning him off to bond with us. I look back and tell my rib she has done an outstanding job, I mean straight Queen power! No Doctor, give me something for the pain, I mean nothing, straight bring our baby in the world! She was glowing in a way I never witnessed her glow before.

We held each other's hand for a moment until the nurse brought Jaishaun over. For any man or woman, as parents this is when time freezes.

The moment when you are looking into your child's eyes for the first time and you feel something for someone else in the world, stronger than you have ever felt in your life.

We both zoned out and got lost in Jaishaun's presence with us whispering our own aspirations in his ear. We soak in a few more "lost in his eyes" moments as the new family that we are and the nurses began to get Mom and Baby together to transport them into a private room. Unfortunately, at the time in Kings County Hospital private accommodations involved another Mom or two in the same room that was as private as it was going to get. As Mom & Baby make their way to the room, I detour to the family in the waiting room to let them know Baby Boy is in the world safely.

As I gave hugs and engaged in some powerful convo with the family, I began to feel like something was nudging me. I couldn't help but feel like I needed to get back to Baby Boy. I took the cue to go back as my cousin Red shares with me "You a man now, take care of your Baby Boy".

I won't ever forget the abundant amount of love, high-powered energy and great feeling of power that was running through my veins as I was walking through the hallway on the way back to them. As soon as I got back to the room I noticed a concerned look on my rib's face. When I come in the doctors are telling her that Jaishaun had to be admitted into NICU. NICU is the Neonatal Intensive Care Unit. The doctor and nurse began to explain to us what is going on and this is where my fatherhood journey really begins!

The Doctor begins to further explain that not only does Jaishaun have a heart murmur (*which is a small hole in his heart*); he has slight tremors and jaundice. During the doctor going into detail he then asked if my rib drank or smoked during the pregnancy, which I could attest to: she was never a smoker or drinker period, and definitely not during the pregnancy. So, in this moment when I was smoking and drinking leading up to my rib getting pregnant was on me. This is one of those moments where my newborn Son may be experiencing disruptive things in his life as a result of choices I made in my own life thus far. I later learned from the doctor that either parents partaking in bad habits including a bad diet could be a contributing factor to Jaishaun being diagnosed with these conditions.

*Now in this moment could I offer you this, although I shared with you how prepared I thought I was for bringing a child into this world and raising the child as we should. Just know that living and breathing the decisions of having a child is a totally different animal than just the warm fuzzy feelings you get imagining it.*

The doctor finishes the conversations by telling us what is going to be done and what we could expect. In Jaishaun's case the few days he would be in the NICU, he would have to undergo more tests to see the seriousness of the heart murmur. For the first few days he would also be in an incubator that would help with his acute jaundice and that hopefully his tremors would subside the more he gets adjusted in the world. After the news was given to us they excused themselves from the room giving us time to make a few decisions regarding Jai.

Of course after the conversation finished my rib and I had to shift through the tears that were swimming down our faces, thinking we both just shared our first heavy experience in our lives as Parents. We don't want to feel like this regarding our first moments with our child. Why is this happening? What can we do? What can I do?

We both decided on focusing energy on making sure that whatever is in our power to do, we have an obligation to do it. At that very moment I got a glance as to the type of Father I needed to become as well as the growing I had to do as a man. Not only was my son now the reason I had to make stronger decisions but also my rib was looking to me now more than ever.

The next day I leave work to go straight to the hospital. Again the feeling of where is my baby boy is overwhelming and I arrive to see my rib in a space that says nothing of happiness. She begins to cry, sharing with me that she only saw him once, they didn't let her feed him and he has a patch of hair cut out. Before this experience I can say some things I was passive about in my life but it was a different feeling emerging in regards to the care of our little prince.

I asked my rib what was the nurse's name and told her I would be right back I'd see what's going on. As I began to make my way to the nurses station one of them started staring me down crazy like I didn't belong there. I respectfully ask for the nurse my rib had been communicating with and with attitude in tow she asks "What baby are you here for?" I let her know which Baby and the reason I'm asking in addition to why no one is communicating with my rib in regards to our child.

I respectfully began to let her know just because I appear to be a young man and you may not have seen many young brothers in here during this process or take any accountability in this stage, it is going to change today you have met a young man who you will have to learn how to deal with because everyone is to be held accountable for my child despite how you may feel about me or my rib.

I was met with complete silence for a few seconds and then the Nurse expressed her thoughts in a not so professional manner. During the time the Nurse decided to express her thoughts my parents started to arrive. As the Nurse continued to get a little more out of her character, I lost it! Never had I been in a position where I felt I was speaking for someone who had not yet had a voice to speak. As I looked through the glass where the babies laid in their incubator, every other baby was together but mine.

I felt like they see a young couple and think that we can't articulate or are not worthy of the same respect as an older couple would receive. Who would allow things to be done to their child without their knowledge and be ok with it? Not us!

As I expressed this still in a respectable tone, one of my dads grabbed me and asked me to calm down. I immediately ask one of them "If it was me, would you be calm. Would you allow this type of treatment to happen to me and not say anything?" And that was the very moment my fathers looked me in the eyes as if they understood where I was coming from. They understood that I was only acting as a concerned Father would and began to ask the same questions.

As one of my aunts walked back with me to the room to tell my rib what was going on I couldn't help but to have an overwhelming feeling of purpose. As I tell my rib what took place and wait for further explanation as to why our son was not bathed and the missing patch of hair on his scalp a Doctor walks in the room. The Doctor begins to apologize for the lack of communication and shares that they intended no malice to our son or us. As for the missing patch of hair, he shared they were taking further tests for Jaishaun's heart murmur and there were no veins available except the one they saw in his scalp, therefore the reason for the missing patch. The reason they didn't share this with my rib was because they were taking the test in the early morning and the necessity of obtaining some results were cause for immediate action.

Both my rib and I expressed our concerns as well and the Doctor assured us that there was nothing to worry about; Jaishaun was being bathed as we speak and his test results indicated that we could take him home with a heart monitor for a few days. The heart monitor was just an extra precaution to make sure that it was something that Jai could possibly grow out of.

I believe this to be one of the great examples of the extremes that you can encounter as a Parent. A few hours before this I would not have imagined that I would be in this hospital ready to hold any and everyone accountable for their actions in regards to dealing with my child and handling something of this magnitude.

This was fatherhood 101; you contributed to bringing him in the world. Now, you have to contribute to his well being now that he is in the world.

We are told what this experience may feel like. You see movies; you may see live examples of what being a Father is like, but until you actually breathe, feel and live, being a Father, to be a parent will never fully be understood until that very moment your experiencing it. When your day-to-day now includes decisions that have everything to do with the way your child lives, you are now a full-fledged Father.

# BREATHING BEING
# A FATHER

*"Hello young people, I am Dr. Tyrone Tucker I have great news for you, your son Jaishaun is going to be going home today. All of his test results came back and besides monitoring his heart murmur, we believe this young baby is strong enough to go home with Mom and Dad".* Let me tell you, those were the most exciting words my rib and I could hear, at the same time I thought the nervousness was over when I saw my son come into the world from out of my rib, but nope it was just the beginning.

To be a 1000% honest I was more nervous then my rib as we were preparing to bring our son home for the first time. Nurturing comes easy to her; she oozes "I take care of my baby". On the other hand, I had thoughts like "How do I do this and am I ready to handle this?" I had questions upon questions. I was way past the "can I handle it" stage.

Our little man was here. There was no time to get lost in myself trying to answer these questions when our son needed me to move in real time.

As I snap out of my "Can I do it right?" vibes my rib was in full go mode. She begins taking out the fresh onesies, his 1$^{st}$ outfit and his handsome baby tools like his baby wave brush. I glance at her and see that mommy glow all over her face. To all my soon to be Dads or freshly new Dads you will know or learn what I'm talking about.

The moment of truth is here, they bring Jaishaun in the room to us and Mama is in full love my baby mode. I go into presidential security mode, thinking about the ride home, got to make sure the car seat is secured right, make sure no air hit his baby nostrils. It's cold outside, nobody better touch him, and I mean all types of top tier bodyguard things are running through my mind. I thought to myself that raising a child does come with more than changing diapers, burping and feeding them. We have a whole human we are responsible for now.

The way he speaks, what he eats, what his diet is, him learning how to use the potty and the numerous obligations that come with having a child begins to rattle you a bit. I'm very transparent in omitting this now but then I thought, "Where is the guidebook?" The little hand I did have in helping raising my brothers and sisters was nothing compared to the huge hand I have in raising my son. I change a few diapers as an older brother, but they are two different realities when it comes to helping with a child and raising your own child.

As we got ready to make our way out of the hospital to our way home, the previous Nurse whom I had the words with during Jaishaun's stay in NICU came to my rib and I and said she wanted to wish us all the blessings in the world. Although we did not meet on good terms, she wanted us to know that she does respect us as young parents. The Nurse asked us to promise her that we would continue to strive and be the best Parents we can possibly be.

After the Nurse left the room my rib and I looked at each other, surprised, and one of my 1$^{st}$ lessons as a Father was revealed to me, which was: we must fight and stand up for our child needs consistently, regardless of how anyone feels or his or her opinion. What matters as a Father and a Mother ultimately is how our decisions will shape their very ideas, morals, and knowledge in character that will help them stand on a solid moral presence.

Baby diapers: check. Baby formula: check. Baby heart monitor: check. We were given a crash course on how to use it and what to watch for. All things that Baby needs, "You better grab it babes" my rib said as we were exiting the room where we had become full-fledged Parents. As we were making our way home, I wasn't sure if it was the blood that splashed in my eye a few weeks ago from Jai's birth that altered my vision or his birth itself but the world didn't seem the same to me.

Driving through the streets of Brooklyn on our way home, I began to see a colder side to the world. The thoughts began to cross my mind now, like "You were out here surviving this on your own, but now you have two additional people whose well being you have to consider." Again, gentlemen, the loving part to make the Babies we all enjoy and are easy, but are you ready for the part that turns you into a full fledged Father -- cause that happens whether you are ready or not.

Although my mind has spun into a sort of frenzy, our 1$^{st}$ night home with our son as a family was nothing like anything I felt before. My rib and I weren't playing house anymore: this was real. Most of the first moments home were learning together things we didn't know as Parents like how to read the heart monitor. The other portion was my rib and I taught each other things we may have not known before this. I was so proud to be a Dad I was reading everything from the right way to change a diaper to the benefits of breastfeeding your child. Fellas, if this route is chosen which I highly suggest because of the benefits it offers our children, remember the "bobbies" bottles are the Babies. You have to share!

At this very moment I like to make a clear distinction of what I was feeling and the thoughts on my mind may not cross every man's mind who is a Father to be, or that is already a Father. I think this is the difference in when a Man decides if he is just a contributor to the birth of a child versus being the keeper of the child. Every man may not be designed to be the Father that his child needs. Some of us have to take an honest look at who we are as Men and really evaluate whether we should become Fathers.

I can honestly say I was ready to endure anything Fatherhood would throw at me. Not knowing what was going to be thrown at me and understanding the type of Man I had to become would be the things that were new to me. Some of the first nights Jaishaun was home from the hospital were some of the scariest nights of my life. Not because I wasn't capable of taking care of him, but because taking care of Jaishaun was new to us. In some of our first experiences with us being home, if it were one concept I had to absorb fast it would be patience! Not just me, but all Fathers need to absorb this fast.

I'm sure we all heard the stories where some parents lose it, harming their child because their child may have been crying all night and the parent doesn't know why.
I'm proud to say that the love and small patience at the time never brought me to harming any of my children till this present day. Through my first-born Son I learned to understand the value in having patience for him, but also the value of patience that was in it for me. Through patience I learned more understanding. A child is new to the world. Things that are elementary and or easy to us are grad school to them. It is we, their parents that they depend on to navigate them through this world we brought them into.

Take the example of crying. Some babies that I know have had a cool baby persona. Not too much crying if at all and very calm until they feel their needs are not being met and even in that space they remain cool. Some babies on the other hand know their communication is through crying. That doesn't make that child a brat or a bad child. It is just the child using the tools they have to communicate their needs or that something is wrong.

The beautiful journey about parenting is through our newly acquired patience we get the privilege to learn how to teach our child to communicate. If we pay close attention you began to learn that cry may mean, "Aye Mama, this milk is too hot", or "Dad, I just let go this load in my diaper that doesn't feel right on my buns, can you get it off me?"

As our first days began to turn into weeks and then months with our first-born my natural Father instincts began to reveal itself. A month after Jaishaun's birth and a few doctor visits later the heart monitor was gone, along with the heart murmur. Changing Jaishaun diapers, getting his bottle together and knowing what cries represented specific needs of his were becoming more natural to us. I can't help but to tell you this was some of the most life changing experiences in learning to raise my child, but taking care of him would be what would constantly run in my mind.

Getting a job was never much of a problem for me. When I locked in on something that I want, it would be mine, I wouldn't stop until the goal was achieved. With Jaishaun being born, I had a new resource of over achiever juice that I had tapped into.

I began working several jobs at a time, losing some to bullshit and moving through others to get to a better one, to become a better provider. To tell you I was a squeaky clean guy would be a little distant from the truth. And although I was working I kept a few fingertips in the concrete with the hopes of my music career blasting off at some point and allowing me to leave behind anything that would jeopardize my freedom or wellbeing.

In all honesty the younger years of my son's childhood is when I began to have the biggest battle within myself. Before Jaishaun's birth my rib stayed with a job, but we both came to an agreement that I would bring home the clams and she would nurture our son. I had no problems at all with this but I guess at the time the universe wanted to show me that something's don't go as planned.

Even though I had a decent job at the time, I was feeling the pressure of making sure I provided for my family so I wanted more… and that more led me to putting more than my fingertips in the concrete. Certain things I made sure to stay away from, but the things I did decide to get involved with -- I was all the way in. This is where my mind began to play tricks on me. At the time what I thought was going to make me be a better provider for my family actually started to slowly pull me away from them. I never negated my fatherly duties, but my non-presence at home began to take a toll on them both.

I shared this because it speaks to the lifestyle choices we tend to make as men that affects us and our household but the pursuit of providing can often blind us to the dangers we subject ourselves to. Not only did I begin to see the effects it was having on my rib, but I also started to see the effects it had on our son. I began to learn that as a Father yes I had to provide for my family but the manner in which I was doing so was very important for all of our well beings.

As Jaishaun began to get older I really began to see how my movements affected him. Not by just the results of my actions but also the fact that I am "The Man" to my son. So therefore any and all moves his dad makes: He is watching.

Although I began rebuilding a relationship with my biological father and having a bond with my stepdad (*I never refer to him as my stepdad, just want to offer clarity*) there was never a blueprint of "fatherhood" that I had to refer to raising my son. Throughout my childhood I learned things from these men in my life but it was more about the type of man I should become.

Raising my son on a day-to-day basis was something I had to learn to do in my own right. The only thing I could use as reference points were from the few moments I had with my father in my childhood as well as the things Poppa Doc would instill in me when I was a young teenager. I said to myself that I'm in a position to offer my son or any other children I was blessed with a side of fatherhood I haven't personally experienced. With the utmost respect to my fathers, it was my mother's way of parenting that I relied on a lot to shape some of my ideals of the type of Father I would become.

Let's be clear: I do agree with the mantra that a woman cannot teach a boy how to be a man. But I do agree that a woman can raise a man. My mother taught me gentleman's etiquette, i.e. putting down the toilet seat, opening the doors for a young lady, etc. It is your dad who teaches you how to hold yourself when using the bathroom. It is your dad that teaches you the charismatic words you say to a young lady when opening the door for her and pulling out her chair. It is supposed to be your dad that teaches you how to defend yourself and help boost your confidence; it's an extreme difference.

Only a few of us are blessed in a manner where some of these things are known to us without the experience of it being taught, but not every young man is afforded that blessing.

Reflecting back on early days as a Father I see some of the mistakes I made. I also see some of my greatest moments in my fatherhood experiences as well. When Jaishaun was around five or six years old I was making the transition from leaving the streets alone and really learning the business of music. I still thought I can ride the fence of the streets and become a legitimate businessmen, but a few experiences that Jaishaun had because of the way I was living began to change my mind of trying to balance street life and a businessmen life.

We as Fathers have to make the choice sooner than later, knowing that our child's life depends on it, so it should be sooner or you will not be afforded a later.

One of the biggest reasons for me sharing this memoir was to do what life experience did for me... show me the consequences of my choices in real time. It is my hope that any story or experience I have shared in this memoir can encourage or inspire the next young man who is becoming a Father, to start on a righteous path to stand on and become the great Fathers our children need.

I'm not proud of this at all, and still thank GOD till this day from saving my son from the realities of my life. Living in Brownsville, Brooklyn made me decide that I was not going to be preyed on or taking advantage of. In most cases when you are living like this young men tend to carry or own guns. I was hustling, dabbling in a few things so I used to have several "tools" for the street trade I was involved in. Now please understand my perspective on fire-arms was not like little boys viewed them as toys.

Through one of my older male influences I was taught to respect firearms, how to care for them, that loss of life can and will happen if not handled responsibly. This is another example of how a Father's presence can have an impact on our young sons as well. If we are taught the right way, we will not exercise the wrong actions.

It was a nice spring afternoon as I remember it and I was moving on the day busting a few moves while my rib was in the throne with Jaishaun. About 2 hours or so goes by and I get a call from my rib telling me I need to come home immediately. When I arrive I see the closet door open, my rib is shaking her head pointing at one of my shoeboxes and then proceeds to let go on me. "Babe you can't have these things in the house we have a Son now. He found it in the closet and good thing something about it scared the shit out of him because he left it there on the floor"... I could tell y'all the rest of what my rib was saying but just know she was extremely upset and to be honest I couldn't remember what she was saying because this wild feeling that I can't describe came over my body.

I stared at my son for what seemed like a few minutes just thinking if anything were to happen to him especially of this nature, this is something that as a man I wasn't quite sure I could live with.

I snapped out of it when Jaishaun came to me and grabbed my face. Now although I had engaged the safety and put it somewhere I thought was out of his reach, this experience showed me that when we choose to keep something in our lives we are not the only one affected by the results of that choice.

I knew a few young men and heard a few stories where no safety or concern was practiced in the household and as a result some young children, as well as adults didn't have a good outcome. This was a mistake that I immediately learned the lesson from and was thankful that it was just that.

I began to examine my fatherhood position a lot more and thought to myself I need to do a lot better by my son.

It was my choice to live the way I was living and at this point in my son's life I was making choices for him that he had no control over yet, it could make or break him. For sometime I was very upset with myself and from that day forward I vowed that I would never endanger my child or my rib's life like that again.

As I share and reflect on this incident I see referring to yourself as a "Man" yet not moving like one in all aspects of your life are things we have to take control of as Men. I really started to think that being 19 years old, having an apartment and a child with my rib was not the only thing that solidified me as a Man or a Father. It was how I led my family; it was about how I began to take care of them in a manner that was worthy of being called a Father. Being a Father is more than conceiving a child with a woman and coming home to a space you called your own. Being the man I needed to be and the Father I wanted to be was going to have to start with my perspective, the way I see things, I had to evolve.

Up until I had my son I had to let go of the circumstances I thought was molding me to be the man I was at that time. I was never a man that felt he had to prove anything to anyone. I was a man who dived all the way into things and because I grew up in the surroundings I did, I began to adopt the ways of surviving the streets. In all honesty, some of these ways are why I am here today sharing this memoir. It is a lot of the foolish ideals of the street that I dropped, which is the very reason I'm here today as well.

For the most part at this time in my life I was fighting for control of my manhood. I'm speaking of actually controlling my thoughts and actions as a man. See in my opinion when a young man grows up without his father present in some of the most impressionable years of his life, where will he get the basic concept of what being a man is about? When there is no one who you can tailor your steps after, when there is no example of how and why things should be done in a certain manner guess who decides for that young man...the streets, and what society portrays to us is where impressionable young men will get their ideals of being a man whether it be right or the wrong way of life.

It was clear to me that I wasn't a follower. I just needed to move in every realm of a real man and that's thinking for myself first. Learning that the next man's circumstances or ideals are not mine. If I didn't start to exhibit more of this in my life, someone else would dictate my life along with my son's for the lack of me standing on my own choices and that is not a man. The reality of life is that everything is not for everybody. Some paths that one man takes or chooses may not be the correct routes for the next man. Understanding and learning what is for you and the path you choose in life is what manhood is about. Before you can learn to love and care for someone else you have to do that for yourself. Before you can teach and guide someone else you have to learn to teach and guide yourself.

Of course some of us develop these strengths and character traits early on in our life giving our upbringing or based on who has contributed and or guiding our lives. Some things are taught and some things are learned through experience. When you become a Father the ways in which you were taught to be a man and carry yourself is what you will naturally depend on to raise your child.

Again I realized my blessings in regards to being taught a moral compass and the measure of a man is in his actions. A man is measured in how he takes care of his family. My grandmother Annie Mae, my mother's Mom always demanded that her grandsons carried themselves as respectable upstanding men. My great Grandfather Sharpie was another elder in my life who demanded I present and move like a strong, intelligent young man should and he always let me know anything other then that is not a man. My mom required that I be held accountable for my actions and with doing so I would understand that the choices I made would affect my life, so the foundation was built in me on many levels, minus it coming from my father.

I'm sure this is the part where some may feel I had some type of guidance through the other people in my life and that may very well be true. But the first time interacting and engaging with my son in the beginning stages of his life was something I could not pull from experience. So, I began to see that what might have been a lack of in my life; I had the opportunity to offer that to my son abundantly. I began to give my son the things I had not experienced with my father at a young age and that began to become my tutorial book to raising my son.

When having a child or children I believe two things happen to us. Either we become a better person because of the life we bring in the world or we remain the same because we don't know the importance of who we have now become to another human being.

I am forever in debt to my first-born son because his existence teaches me so many things about what manhood really is. I may have been angry with my father for him not being there in my early childhood, but I was never bitter. I accepted when I was young that my dad chose the path he chose and that had nothing to do with me.

It had to do with the type of man he chose to be at that time in his life. The blessings of being able to make the man choice to raise my son from the beginning as I should, showed me that I had the opportunity to build something my dad might not have been able to see at that moment in his life.

A little before my son was born my dad & I reconnected when I ran away from home and in that time I shared with him we came to terms with what transpired in our relationship. I learned a few lessons during this very critical time in all of our lives. I say critical because my father is our senior and for as much as we think we needed him he needs us in his life as well. In his own transitions he was going through as a man battling his own demons, he found more strength in having a Son who continued to love him despite the mistake that he made not being there early on in my adolescent life.

In this particular part of my life I was learning that I was the bridge between generations. Me having a relationship with my father is my son having a Grandfather present and eventually my son building a direct relationship with him. Through me standing in who I am as a man, I am able to offer my sons some of the countless blessings I have in my life. In times I didn't have my dad to go to, I had my grandfather or a respected male figure to keep me in line. Who was I to deny that to my sons based on my past?

This is why I share with you all I had to get my manhood back. I was not going to allow society to tell me to be a broken man because I didn't grow up with my dad on a day to day. Being a broken man because the portrayal of men holding down households wasn't many and a man carrying himself, as a man under God's laws were not often an example to our peers and I during our adolescence. I'm very thankful for "Poppa Doc" because in a time in my life where the edge of the cliff was on either side of me, he really gave me the jewels and allowed me to take what I knew would make me a better man.

Let's be clear when I was younger "mucking up" as my mom would say, he was a man of less alphabets and more action. His action more or less would show me how a man was supposed to handle things.

Life changing lessons are revealed to us when we are ready to see them and not a moment sooner. I began to see that through-out our lives continually growing as men is a duty in life. Some instances in our lives may afford us the opportunity to be great or stay in our mediocrity. In order for knowledge and growth to be gained, mistakes must be made and we must find the teachable moment in it. In those teachable moments we must also come to know that lessons are not just learned from the students perspec-tive but it is very possible for the teacher to learn from the stu-dent as well.

Praises due! Because I realize now that that the man I aspire to be would only happen by the things I would endure on my journey being a Father. When we look to become something in our life take for example, someone who wants to be a Doctor. The major part of the journey to becoming a Doctor requires a lot of study-ing. At some point the knowledge has to be applied or practiced, but even though there has been much knowledge acquired to be a Doctor, I'm sure you would agree the most important experience would be gained when the Doctor is in action. Then a skill is de-veloped and grows on many levels based on applying the know-ledge, putting it to use and practicing it.

Fatherhood or parenting can be viewed in the same respect. I went through my own moments growing up as a young man try-ing to find my way. As I was growing up what my parents taught me would ultimately be my guide and help me navigate in the adult world but I would have to take what was given and the knowledge I was acquiring to build myself to the man I wanted to become. I believe the same to be with parenting. Our children become some of our best students as well as some of our best teachers.

Being a Father day in and day out is my fatherhood textbook. Even if my dad were present in my younger years, who's to say that would have made me the greatest Dad ever? It may have served me better and it may have saved me some growing pains, but my son's existence is what challenged me to bring the man I wanted to be out and the Father I aspired to be to the forefront of all of our lives. When we are living our lives childfree or even living single we only require concern for ourselves. Some adults don't even exhibit concern for themselves let alone for a child.

It's not up to any of us to decide for someone else if they are ready to be a parent. You have to want to be a parent. I endured some of the things I did because I wasn't going to give up on being the best Father I could possibly be to my son. To say your child comes first and to actually put them first are entirely two different things. There was nights that my son's belly trumped my hunger pains. It was days where my rib and I could not think of indulging in things we may have wanted to do because it would take away from Jaishaun and as I was becoming the Father I wanted to be, it's unacceptable for my son to do without the necessities. For a young parent whether you're a Mother or a Father that is not something that comes easy for anyone.

My son taught me how to be patient. My son taught me how to be thorough. If it is one person who taught me how to speak up and articulate things that needed to be communicated, understood and respected coming from a man, it was my son. That was one of the first lessons I learned from his birth at the hospital. I was not supposed to be silent and wait or allow anything to happen to him. I had to learn how to ask questions and understand that it is very much my right as a Father to concern myself with everything regarding my son. Learning how to communicate effectively is vital because we become their voices until they are communicating effectively on their own.

My son's existence helped me bring what already existed in me as a Father to light. When I thought of some of the personal experiences that I really thought changed me and defined me as a man, this really helped me to understand being a Father is about the sacrifices we are willing to make. Fatherhood is about the foundations that we ourselves stand on: our morals, purposes, and way of living really dictate the path we lay for our children's life because it has the potential to affect them in every way possible.

In some stories, brothers talk about what they were involved with in the streets and boast. My decision to be involved in the streets was always to support the real responsibilities that I had as a young man like rent, investing in my business, my bills and having a young thunder cat to feed. Nonetheless I decided to get in the trenches with the team heavy.

Of course there was a code that we followed amongst each other and for the most part my stance on that code has been to always honor and show a fellow brother the same, as I would expect for myself.

Anything that I was involved in or contributed to I made sure it was done to the best of my abilities; it was not any different for the streets. At this point in time it was heavy to the point where shootouts and moving "work" in the concrete wasn't something I was experiencing in movies. Who you were and how you got down depended on your survival.

One particular instance out of town with the team, were running around celebrating life before we started the grind day. Weather beautiful, the day moving how we needed it to and during that whole time I felt like something was off. I keep getting this overwhelming vibe like something is not right. I tried to ignore the vibe I was getting as we got further in the day it was time to grind but this feeling was punching me in my gut. It wasn't scary like I have to use the bathroom type of gut feeling. It wasn't the cats that we were feuding with that had me off; this was a super different vibe.

Getting further into the night hustle I push through it but I couldn't ignore this feeling any longer. As we all glide out and convene at headquarters I dipped to the side to get my thoughts together when a warm tingling feeling came over me. Something told me that if I didn't do what I wanted for my life, my life would not be mine. Making this decision to move on my vibe until I figured out what the hell was going on had to be done now. I had to speak to my people as men that were out in the battlefield together. Whether they would respect my decision or not I had to let them know that this is what I had to do as a man, this life wasn't for me.

As I entered the room to speak to my people, I can't remember me being nervous at all. Being a man, doesn't equate to moving on how other people felt about you. I simply told them that this life wasn't for me any longer and if I continued with this life I was going to go deeper than I want to without the chance of coming back. With me being conflicted on what I wanted at this point I didn't want to put anyone's life in jeopardy because of the state I was in.

Not much was said after I spoke on it but this was something I felt I needed to do and I had to do it. That night one of my people was arranging to go back home so I rode out with him. As I rode away I felt like a few bonds might be broken, as well as me not being seen in the same light that I once was but I didn't give a shit. The further I got away from that life and the closer I got to my son, I understood what the vibe I was getting was about. I learned the mistake of not following my gut and it cost me big.

The reason I did these things was to be a Father that provided for his household. Putting myself in situations that would take my freedom away from me would not allow me to be a present Father.  A few short weeks after I decided to bounce from that situation my people were raided. Several of them received some heavy jail time; I'm talking 10 years plus! Any time behind bars is life changing. If I would not have stood my ground I could have been caught up in a situation where it would have definitely taken a toll on my family.

As I reflect on all the times I tried to figure out what was the feeling that had overwhelmed me that day, the only thing I could ever come up with was first, GOD saving me. Second, the fact that I knew what I wanted for my life and the streets were not it. Sometimes we have to do what we have to do to survive, but at what costs? If I continued to live that life I wouldn't have felt anything. The Father in me knew that it wasn't about answering to no one other than self. What words could I find to tell my son that I failed him by losing my freedom or not being there for him the way that I should be.

How would I tell him that because I didn't stick to my own convictions as a man that some of the most important moments of his life I wasn't going to be there because I did not stick to my ideals!

To fail my son would be me failing myself. I would be contributing to the cycle of bringing another child into the world and not being responsible enough to care for him. There has been many ways Jaishaun's existence has taught me that the man I aspired to be was inside of me the whole time. That man emerging to the surface was all about the decisions I would make. They would either reveal the man I wanted to be or a lesser version of that man.

Being a Father is all about living and dedicating yourself to someone other than you. In my journey thus far being a Father I learned early that being selfish is not a good trait for a parent. If you're a man that recognizes you may not have all the patience in the world then guess what, you better acquire some patience quickly.

Let's talk bare logic to being a parent for a moment. A feeling or an emotion sparked in us to have an encounter with another human where we both contribute to a human life. Whether the encounter was planned to lead to childbirth, a moral obligation is now upon both parties to contribute to the life that they have created. This is not passing judgment on anyone but some of us are not built to be a parent, because when the child is here, they do not have the capacity to lead, feed, guide, nurture and care for themselves.

It was the earlier times in my fatherhood journey where I wondered, how the hell am I going to get through this? The first time Jaishaun got sick with fevers, I felt helpless. When medicine is taking its time to work through their system, you want to be sure that you are giving your child the right dose. The child has no clue as to what is going on in the world and they are hollering at the top of their lungs. It isn't about how much noise they are making, but how uncomfortable they are.

We could be told how these experiences can shape us as parents, but until you actually are living the experience, the decision has to be made sooner than later what type of parent you will strive to be.

My first born helped me understand that his choice in coming to the world was not his at all. It was my choice and my rib's choice, and it was our duty to honor the choices we made regarding his existence because GOD gave us that responsibility. Those choices wouldn't only be important in his beginning stages of his life but up until he became the adult we raised him to be to make his own choices regarding his life. I must admit that in the early stages of Jaishaun's life I was still getting myself together as a man. As I began to engulf myself into the role as a Father the more I had to make clear decisions on how we would raise our son.

This led me to make one of the most important decisions in all of our lives. Jaishaun was just turning 6 years old and I had just dodged a heavy felony charge -- thank God -- and I was under heavy pressure to do right by my family. I agreed with all of the advice that was given to me by my family: It was only a matter of time where hustling hard like this was going to end one or two ways. My rib has never shown any signs that she would leave me before, but this time she told me I had to make a decision...it was either her and our son or the streets. If I chose the streets it was time for her to go because this was not the life she envisioned for us and definitely wasn't the life she wanted to raise our son in. She expressed to me that my son did not deserve to be like some children she knew whose Mothers would take them to see their dads in jail. I never wanted that for any of us and she was a thousand percent correct.

This hit me really hard. Not only was my rib expressing the way she felt but several other people, including my parents, aunts and a few close friends did as well. I digested all the conversations and knew that I would have to do better and do what I knew was right. Me running in the streets, while at the same time building a career in music was coming to a fork in the road. I had to choose between one road or the other, and I had to choose fast.

As I was reflecting deep into what I needed to do as a man I'll never forget this moment... my grandma Charlotte (may she rest in peace) called a meeting at her house to speak to the family. Now I had one on one building sessions with her from time to time but never with the family. During the meeting my Grandma took the time to address everyone and gave her raw opinion on what each family member needed to do to get themselves together. I'm thinking I'm just here to bear witness...nope. It was my turn and my grandma simply says to me you need to do right by the family you help create. She couldn't tell me what I needed to do -- she said I needed to figure it out, but this life doesn't need to be here in NYC. She suggested I go stay with my uncle Frank (R.I.P) out in Maryland and build a life that my family and

I would be proud of. After the family meeting, I went back home and shared with my rib what took place and what was said. She asked what were we going to do, I told her I wasn't sure. Looking back at this moment, I was looking for excuses to stay in NYC not seeing that maybe another surrounding may offer me the chance to build the life I wanted. I took my time, thinking, "I'll be good; I don't need to bounce anywhere." Then it happened!

It's an early sunny afternoon in Brooklyn; it was just turning 12pm... Jaishaun and I are relaxing at the house. He asks if I can take him to the store and I tell him to suit up so we can go. We stroll out from our basement apartment to the bright sun and Jai's face lit up.

We exit the gate and if you're from Brownsville, Brooklyn, like me you know things can get crazy in a millisecond. I got this vibe and I grabbed Jaishaun's hand as we hit the corner. With the store in sight, I see one of our OG's Mr. Wilson (may he rest in peace) walking towards Jaishaun and I. We don't get within handshake distance from each other before I hear some yelling behind me then I hear shots going off. Were talking in broad daylight: Kids, Grandmas, and the Postman are outside and it's getting funky immediately. As I turn around I snatch up Jaishaun in my arms and run towards one of my people's porch that was in the opposite direction of where the shooting was going down.

When we get to the stoop, Mr. Wilson is in the gate with us and asks if we're good. I tell him "Yes, no one is hit." When we look down the block we see a young dude laid down on the sidewalk a block away. As I turn back around to make sure Jaishaun is good, this look of scared confusion takes over his face. It was that moment that I knew It was time for me to do everything in my power to give my son a better life. I let things cool off for a bit before taking him to the store and in that moment I decide it's time for me to expand the horizons for my family. It was time for me to move out of NYC.

This wasn't about me not being able to handle the environ-
ment I was raised in because I became immune to the senseless
shit that goes on in our urban communities. This was about my
son becoming immune to the senseless violence that goes on in
these urban communities, and I wouldn't subject my child to this.
Enough was enough! Now let's be very clear, violence takes place
everywhere. It was just time that I offered my family and myself
an opportunity better than the circumstances of our current en-
vironment.

Striving to be a better man myself, I didn't want to feel that there
was no other way. I couldn't be stubborn to my ideals and allow
my son to not have a better perspective of life offered to him.
Being a Father now, I had to examine the world in a way where
it wasn't about what the world offered me, but what the world
would offer my son. As a Father, how could I position my son to
gain everything he aspired to be in life, how can I show him that
he is not what society tells him he is based on what we see in our
neighborhoods, entertainment and social media? It clicked in my
mind that I have to lead my son by example. It was necessary that
I show him his life matters more than anything I have ever desired
in life because that's what being a Father is.

Through me becoming a better man, I put my son on a path to
be a greater man than I am. This is the thin line we all walk when
becoming a Father and deciding to be an active Father, not just
a sperm donor. The unfortunate reality is a sperm donor is all
some of us will ever be... We are giving the free will to procreate.
That does not mean everyone accepts the responsibility of being
a Father or Parent.

Before the birth of my son and due to my own experiences with
my father, I can honestly say I had a desire to be a Father. Did
I think it was going to be easy? No, not at all. I knew I would
be tested. I knew sacrifices would challenge me to build a relationship and an understanding with a woman to where we work

together to raise our son the best way we could. Not every situation is a man blessed with a woman who doesn't play games or use their child as a pawn. Not every situation is a woman blessed with a man who is going to do what he must to honor his fatherhood.

In these experiences I shared with you throughout this memoir, I give examples on how my son's existence shaped my fatherhood to become stronger. Jaishaun being in my life is what enhanced my experience and knowledge as a Father.

Although I contributed to the creation of another human with my rib, ultimately the bond I needed to establish with my child had to be through my direct interaction with him. When I decided to move out of town I would be lying to you if I didn't acknowledge I was a bit nervous to go somewhere else I had not been to establish a progressive, stable life for us.

What I can say is it was the overwhelming desire not to fail him that got rid of any doubt or nervousness that I had. I believe as Fathers when you hear your child's heartbeat, you see their smile, you hold their little feet, you witness them come into the world and any man who understands why GOD gave him this power to procreate, does everything in his power to live up to their ideals of being a Father.

Writing this memoir has allowed me to see the situations I never thought I would make it out of. It also showed me the resilience, determination and drive I have acquired to be not only the best Father I could be, but also be the best man I could possibly be. Even at this very moment this memoir is in your hands, I'm still not perfect. I'm still learning through my other two children. I'm still learning through my firstborn son. As he's making his transition into adulthood, I continue to learn how to be a great Father to him and now his siblings.

If we were afforded a moment to reflect on where we used to be in life and where we are currently in life, some of us would change a lot of things. Since writing this and having the fatherhood experience conversation with several brothers of all different generations and cultures, they ask me if I could, would I change the way things played out? I honestly say no; this is what GOD intended. My circumstances and the way things played out was the only way I would become the man I am today.

# I OFFER YOU THIS

When I thought of writing this memoir, it was not my intention at all to write a literal tutorial book on how to be a Father. The intention of this memoir is to share with men who are becoming Fathers, or who are current Fathers, some of the commonalities we face as men. I felt compelled to offer some type of insight through my fatherhood experiences where it would enhance the conversation of the state of fatherhood. The importance of fatherhood extends way past Father's Day or child support. We, as a culture, have suffered generations because the ideals of fatherhood have been lost.

It may seem that our culture is the only culture plagued by fatherlessness, but it's not. I had the opportunity to speak with people from different cultures, different ages, different ethnicities and different genders. Fatherhood issues affect all cultures; it is just depicted as our culture that spearheaded the "fatherlessness campaign". We have many examples of men who offer our culture as well as their family an image and presence of men that we are proud of.

I want to take the time to congratulate and salute the men who overcame the odds they faced growing up without a Father to be the best Father they can be to their Children. It's no secret that there has been an agenda for some time for the destruction of full family households where the Mother and Father are both present, everything from wars, to drugs, to social ploys to destroy the unions that build these strong households were our children benefit from having both parents. It's socially acceptable for a man to be absent from the household. Between "Baby Daddy Syndrome" and "I don't need him to raise my kids", the only one that suffers is the child.

I promise you I am not passing judgment on anyone. We have both been brainwashed to accept ideologies that do not serve the preservation and building of our existence. Some adults have no desire or intention to be a present parent. We have been under siege on so many levels that it has not just affected us mentally, but also spiritually broken some of us. We have to also acknowledge that economics also has been a major component in some Fathers being present in the home.

A Father not having the means to take care of his family can take a toll on a man. This toll has cost some men their freedoms or their life because of minimal resources available to them to maintain and contribute to the household. Unfortunately this has led to many Fathers forfeiting their position because they may feel less than a man. In the world we now live in I think this has shown itself on many levels.

In order for us to begin to build stronger families that raise bright, intelligent, compassionate, human beings -- as well as strengthen the families who exhibited these qualities already, we will continue to create family trees that bare progressive fruit. Fatherhood experiences should be celebrated as a gift and should be respected as such. As I continue my fatherhood journey I am blessed to know that the experience I have obtained in regards to being a Father can now be passed on in time when my children bare their children, GOD willing.

As Fathers, our responsibilities continue throughout our children's adulthood. Even for young men who are not my own, I can share as a man with them that postpartum syndrome is a real thing that your lady can possibly be affected by. If so, it may be times your lady is not in the right mind space to take care of your child and you may have to take the lead and care for your newborn baby -- but you may also have to nurture your lady. Without any discussion or supportive resource a young man, or any man for that matter, may not know that postpartum is not a personal vendetta against the Father. This comes with the nature of bringing children into the world. This is why us as men have to be more invested in our children and our families.

We cannot allow lack of knowledge along with society ideals to project the type of man you need to be for your family. Making sure the health of the woman who brings your children in the world is as important. Your child feels the energies of you both; the child shares the mixture of both your blood and genetics so the well being of you both is the well being of the child.

No statistics are needed to tell you how we all suffer when the man who had a role in bringing you into the world is not there to guide, care, raise and teach you. I could overwhelm you with the hundred of thousands if not millions of lost and broken young kings we have out here because some of their fathers fell victim to circumstance and are doing 25 years to life in prison. How some Children wake up to their father being gone because he was murdered in the streets, so they have no idea of what their father smells like or what a hug from him will feel like.

Do you need a statistic to tell you that our culture would be a lot more powerful and fruitful if two parent households are the standard and not an old school memory? This is not a utopian society I'm speaking of. Just the simple logic that if your child was born out of the love that you have for another human, that child now has to become the primary of that love. We have to begin to understand it is our God-given duty to create the preservation and growth of our children whether you are together as a couple or not.

In the same breath, some cards are dealt where the Mother has to single handedly take care of the Children or the Father has to do so, to no fault of their own. Some Fathers are blessed to have a supportive resource that helps them in raising their children and unfortunately some Fathers don't. Some brothers know what their duties are and rise to the occasion regardless of the circumstances that got them in that position.

In this memoir I hope I have offered any young man the courage to become the best man his heart desires. When you make the decision or a choice has given you the blessing of being a Father, Just make sure that you treat that child, or children, that are brought into the world on behalf of your contribution... like the blessings that GOD made them to be. Make sure that you offer that Child or Children all the security, love, patience, knowledge, compassion, discipline, laughter, and energy you have to offer. Please utilize GOD as your source of guidance, strength and faith.

To my son Jaishaun -- who is now 22 years of age, who is a real estate agent and entrepreneur -- I would like to say in front of the world that you coming into the world is one of the best moments of my life and it is a pleasure to see you grow into the man that you are, the man I know you can be, and will be. I am grateful for everyday I can see your rise to greatness. To my youngest son, Keyshawn, I need you to know that your existence showed me more than any of your sibling's birth that GOD is very real. I hope that in every lesson I give to you, you allow the greatness that is within you to breathe revealing the powerful king that you are. Your determination and desire to be a great leader will allow you to live the powerful life you see yourself living.

Since the day you were born the world threw obstacles in your way, and you have turned those obstacles into mere bumps in the road. Your will and resilience has made me one of the proudest Fathers in the world and I continue to look forward to you doing incredible things in this life of ours. To my youngest, my princess, my baby executive of a Daughter... your existence...shows me that a man has to have compassion and righteousness in his heart. I know, as a man protecting the Mother of my children is a responsibility of mine, but now protecting our daughter is an honored duty. It is not only my obligation to raise you to be respected and honored as the woman your mother and I will raise you to be, but to make sure that you will be respected by the world as the QUEEN that you will grow to be!

Lastly to my rib I would like to share with you this... when a man knows what he wants and knows who he is, he will never take for granted the gift he was given and the goddess he was blessed to have beautiful reflections with. In the bond we have built to- gether we have both watched each other grow from adolescence to adults and have been a part of each other's life journey for some time. You continue to inspire me to be the best man I could pos- sibly be not just for you, but to be the best Father ever to our chil- dren. For that you are truly and always my heart.

To all the Fathers, young and old, ... I wish you abundant under- standing, perseverance, patience, strength and courage. May we continue to embody these strong ideals. May we continue to be what our children need us to be. The best tutorial book I've been given has been this life that has been granted to me. I have been blessed with people, experiences and circumstances that have al- lowed me to strive to be an exceptional Father to my children. As men, we all have our own path to walk and as you decide what kind of Father you will be to your children, I implore you to start with what you wanted from your Father. Start with who you are as a man and examine the things that you as a man can offer your child.

In all honesty, when fatherhood feels unknown and dark, because it will at times...allow GOD to be your beacon of guidance and light. So whether you entered fatherhood at 14,15,19, 18, 20 or 42 know that you are now responsible for the child that is now in the world!

First would like to thank everyone who took the time to purchase and read "Fatherhood at 19... No Tutorial Books". Whether it was for you or someone you thought needed to read this I am very appreciative and humbled. Although this is not an intended tutorial book on fatherhood, I pray me offering some of my experiences, thoughts, lessons and perspective on fatherhood could help any man, young or old, any ethnicity or race because it has and does affect us all.

To all the brothers of my culture, I offer you this. We no longer live in the past that created the circumstances we grew up in, so to our futures we have to offer them the best of us, so that they do not suffer any lack there of, because we didn't do our GOD giving duty!

As Ed OG said… "Be a father to your child". Peace and Power!

If you would like to reach out to reach out to me please feel free to do so via email: Fatherhoodat19ntb@gmail.com.

Via social media Twitter, IG, & Facebook @Fatherhoodat19 or @Fatherhoodat19ntb feel free to like, comment or share!

Also feel free to visit our website www.Fatherhoodat19.com for the latest updates, as well as interviews, discussions and other services and products that will keep you up to date with all of the latest news from upcoming Lil Villa Publishing releases.

## Lil Villa Publishing 2021 releases:

*"The Adventures of Juice & Boogs"* (A big brother/little brother adventure empowerment series)
*"Kaka the Super Baby"* (A empowerment series for little girls about an intelligent super hero baby)